THE CASTILIAN CONSPIRACY (SECOND EDITION)

THE UNCENSORED TRUTH ABOUT THE MOST WIDESPREAD OF ALL SPANISH LANGUAGES

ALLAN TÉPPER

TECNOTUR LLC

CONTENTS

The Castilian Conspiracy   v
Acknowledgments   vii
Introduction   ix

1. Languages that predate their respective countries   1
2. Similarity between the Kingdom of Spain and the United Kingdom   3
3. Bilingual dictionaries between different Spanish languages   5
4. Linguistic damage caused by Franco   7
5. Why the language many call "Spanish" must be called Castilian   11
6. Vicente Fox at the Language Congress in Valladolid   15
7. The first Castilian grammar book   19
8. The Royal Spanish Academy and the Vatican   21
9. Andrés Bello's grammar book   27
10. The Chilean law that protects Castilian   29
11. Castilian and the drum   31
12. Myths about the terms castellano and Castilian   33
13. Where Castilian is spoken today   35
14. When it is correct and appropriate to say "Spanish"   37
15. FAQ about Castilian   39
16. MINAM: Myth regarding accentuation of uppercase letters   41
17. Castilian keyboard or Spanish keyboard?   43
18. The superiority of the Spanish keyboard   45
19. Faulty language, defective thought process   49
20. Healthy Castilianization versus Castenglish   53
21. Why the word Internet must treated as feminine   59

22. What the market demands is...	61
23. The danger of English-language software for Castilian-speakers	63
24. Say it in Castilian, say it proudly	73
25. The Castilian alphabet and its pains	75
26. The verb hay: unique in its category	81
27. Jugo or zumo? Papas or patatas?	85
28. The need for bi-regional audiobooks and dubbing	87
29. Latin America, Hispanic America, Ibero-America or what?	91
30. The plural of tú and its respective black hole	95
31. Advantages of treating people as tú	99
32. Does it behoove us to translate proper names?	103
33. Proper names and their allowable spellings	107
34. United States cities and their official spellings in Castilian	111
35. The singular vos	115
36. Why do I accent my last name?	123
37. Happy Birthday is not the same as feliz cumpleaños	125
38. Some dreams come true...	127
About the Author	131
Some other books by Allan Tépper	133
Credits, brands, and disclosures	135

THE CASTILIAN CONSPIRACY
SECOND EDITION

Allan Tépper

THE CASTILIAN CONSPIRACY

The uncensored truth about the most widespread of all Spanish languages

SECOND EDITION

ISBN for the print version: 978-1-7343294-1-4

(The first edition was Copyright 2013.)

Published by Allan Tépper/TecnoTur LLC

Copyright 2019 according to US and international conventions. No part of this book may be reproduced or transmitted without the explicit, written permission from Allan Tépper/TecnoTur LLC, except in the case of brief quotations in reviews, with a link to books.AllanTepper.com or TheCastilianConspiracy.com

ACKNOWLEDGMENTS

Thanks to all who have helped me learn the Castilian language, both officially and unofficially.

Additional thanks to:

- Antonio de Nebrija (1441 – 1522)
- Miguel de Cervantes Saavedra (1547 – 1616)
- King Carlos III (1716 – 1788)
- Andrés Bello (1781 – 1865)
- Ilan Chester (1952 – present)

...for their collaboration in spreading the truth about the Castilian language, each in their unique way.

INTRODUCTION

For those who don't know me yet, I am from the United States and the first language I spoke was English. I was born in the State of Connecticut. However, due to a strange incident related to my grandmother's cat that took place during my childhood, I became intensely interested in the Castilian language, although I didn't yet know its correct name. My parents don't speak it, nor did my grandparents or great grandparents.

The cat incident

When I was eight years old, I was visiting my grandmother's house in an important city in the State of Connecticut, US. While I played in the yard with my younger brother, I saw the next-door neighbor come out to take a walk. The neighbor, a woman of my grandmother's age, had left the door ajar, and she didn't notice when one of my grandmother's three cats went into her house to check it out. I was a shy eight-year-old kid, but I walked up to the woman to inform her (in English, the only language I knew at that time): "Excuse me, but my grandmother's cat just went into your house."

I had no Idea that the woman didn't speak English until she responded in Castilian, which I didn't understand. We spent what seemed to be five full minutes trying to communicate unsuccessfully, when finally the cat exited her house; I pointed to it, and the immediate problem was solved. However, I felt so powerless since I had been unable to communicate with the woman. At that moment, I promised myself to learn that language which was being spoken in my country. That's why I often say that I owe my Castilian to my grandmother's cat.

At 13 years, I had the first opportunity to study Castilian in Connecticut's public schools, although unfortunately they taught its name incorrectly. Three years went by until I heard the correct name (*castellano*/Castilian) for the first time, although without any adequate explanation. Throughout the first years learning the language I began to adore, I was exposed to many regionalisms, many truths, and many myths about it, its name, and its rules. Years later, during my college years in Ithaca, New York, the ATA (American Translators Association) certified me as a translator. In the following decades, various manufacturers have contracted me to translate and localize tech manuals, software, and advertising, although I don't focus on that like many of my friends do.

Why I wrote this book

I don't know you, but I can't and don't tolerate improper or manipulative terminology because I know that *words make worlds* in people's minds. By the same token, I don't tolerate when some individuals declare "rules" about the Castilian language which are really myths. Improper terminology creates a twisted world in people's minds, never mind myths.

Throughout the upcoming chapters, you'll read about many truths, some of which you may know previously and others that will surprise you. You'll also be exposed to related curiosities and proposals I am making. What's my goal? To have people achieve a better understanding about the realities of the Castilian language, both for its speakers and for those who speak other languages, with respect to Castilian. When I point out myths and truths about spelling, grammar, and accent mark rules, my intention is not to replace the many grammar and style books that exist, but only to clarify some common cases where I see that there is so much confusion.

Allan Tépper

1
LANGUAGES THAT PREDATE THEIR RESPECTIVE COUNTRIES

Many of the languages spoken today predate the country where they are primarily associated. Here are some examples:

- In India, multiple official languages are spoken, but none are called "Indian".
- In Iran, the official language is **Farsi** (also known as **Persian**). There is no such thing as a language called "Iranian".
- In Israel, the official language is called **Hebrew**. There is no such thing as a language called "Israeli".
- While the Soviet Union existed, several languages were spoken natively, but none was called "Soviet".

All of this is a preamble for the next chapter, which deals with an important similarity between the Kingdom of Spain and the United Kingdom.

2
SIMILARITY BETWEEN THE KINGDOM OF SPAIN AND THE UNITED KINGDOM

Both the Kingdom of Spain and the United Kingdom are *unified kingdoms*. By that I mean that both were several completely independent kingdoms. Many of them had —and still have— diverse languages.

In the case of the United Kingdom, there are languages like Cornish (*Kernowek* or *Kernewek*), Gaelic, Irish (Irish Gaelic, a Goidelic language), Scots, and Welsh (*Cymraeg* or *Gymraeg*). If people dared to call the English language "UnitedKingdomish" or "UK-ish", there would likely be protests from the speakers of these other languages spoken in the UK.

In the Kingdom of Spain, where the Constitution of 1978 grants authority to its autonomous communities to classify languages as official (as we'll quote ahead in this book), there are various, for example:

- Castilian (the same one many people sadly call "Spanish" or *"español"* as if there were a single Spanish language)
- Catalán
- Euskera (also known as Basque)
- Galician
- Occitans (see comments ahead)
- Valencian (see comments ahead)

Although the Occitans language group is not exclusive to Spain, the Statute of Autonomy of Catalonia of 2006 established the officiality of the Occitans language group in all Catalonia, and was ratified into law by the Parliament of Catalonia in 2010, by which the Occitans language group, in its Aranese variant, was declared co-official in Catalonia, although with its preferential use in the Aran Valley.

Valencian is also now an official language of Spain (no longer considered a dialect of Catalán) and is regulated by the Valencian Language Academy.

The above list of official languages of Spain may be incomplete when you read this book, and excludes the non-official languages.

3

BILINGUAL DICTIONARIES BETWEEN DIFFERENT SPANISH LANGUAGES

Ahead you'll see the covers of two bilingual dictionaries that allow translating between different Spanish languages (Castilian, Catalán, and Euskera/Basque). My friend Enrique López Quesada brought them from Spain for me several years ago, at my request. (Although he's a Spaniard, Enrique currently lives in Guatemala.)

In both cases, the dictionaries make proper reference to Castilian (or its direct translation), since it would be absurd to say "from Catalán to Spanish" or "from Euskera/Basque to Spanish", since we know that they are all official Spanish languages.

4
LINGUISTIC DAMAGE CAUSED BY FRANCO

Francisco Franco (1892-1975) was the Spanish dictator who caused the most recent linguistic damage related to Castilian and its role with its relationship with the other Spanish languages. During Franco's years in power, he made the teaching and public use of the other Spanish languages (beyond Castilian) illegal. He also sent his soldiers to burn books printed in Catalán in bonfires [source: *Catalunya sota el règim franquista* (Edicions Catalanes de París, 1973) by Josep Benet i Morell and the conference *Pompeu Fabra i Poch. Semblança biogràfica* by Joan Solà (IEC, Barcelona, 2006)]... at least those books his soldiers could find. Fortunately the Catalonians were clever and were able to hide some of the books before they could be found and burned. In my opinion, the best term to describe Franco's cruel linguistic mission is *linguicide*, which is derived from *linguistic genocide*.

Franco's main linguicide mission fortunately failed, and today there are now radio, TV, current books and newspapers in several of the other Spanish languages. However, the side effect of his failed mission is the fact that many people on planet Earth unfortunately call Castilian "Spanish". Also, I know a Catalonian guy whose name should be Jordi, but because of Franco's rules, he had to be baptized as "Jorge", which is the Castilian translation of Jordi. His parents promised to call him "Jordi" forever, despite his forced baptism as "Jorge".

Following is an incomplete list of linguistic orders and decrees issued during the Franco regime:

- Order of the Ministry of Justice May 18, 1938, published in the BOE # 577 on May 28 of the same year (available in PDF) which prohibits names not in the *santoral* (official list of saints) and not in Castilian (except for foreigners and those not baptized in the Catholic faith -that may use their own saints or Castilianized names of recognized historical figures-.
- Order of the Ministry of Organization and Trade Union Action of May 21, 1938, BOE # 582 of May 26 (available in PDF), in which any language other than Castilian is prohibited «in titles, registered names, Statutes or Regulations» and in the «assemblies and Boards» of the entities that depend on that Ministry.
- Order of the Ministry of the Interior of March 7, 1941, by which the Regulation for the Internal Regime

and Service of the Telegraph Corps is approved, BOE # 205, of July 24 (available in PNG), for Spain, only Castilian is allowed in telegrams in «clear language» (and to send there is a list of supported languages, among which there are none of the other languages spoken in Spain).

- Orders of May and July 1940 on the use of Castilian in labels, names, brands and others (three standards of the Ministry of Industry and Commerce: omic19400516, omic19400520 and omic19400708).
- Decree June 2, 1944, «Regulation of the Organization and Notary Regime» published in BOE # 189 of July 7, Art. 148, make it clear that all instruments must be in Castilian only (available in PNG).
- Order of April 23, 1941 in which all the films projected are forced to be in Castilian.

According to Bitacora.Jomra.es:

> We must also add the actions of the Directorate General of Press that — constantly and repeatedly— prohibited magazine or newspaper publications that were not in Castilian, everything that was authorized in "other languages" (such as those examples that some put to defend linguistic freedom where there was none) was authorized for a political purpose, not because the norm would result in the publication of writings in languages other than Castilian.

Throughout the years, I have had the pleasure of meeting many Spaniards from different regions of the country, just as I have met many Argentinians (also correctly known as "Argentines"), Colombians, Costa Ricans, Cubans, Dominicans, Guatemalans, Mexicans, Puerto Ricans, Salvadorans, and Venezuelans. I have discovered that it is not enough to meet a single person from a country —or even a single person from a particular city— to know how people from that city or country think about this subject. Every individual is her/his own world, and if we invited two people from the same city, they will frequently argue about linguistic "facts" that they have previously told me and turn out to be contradictory. Regardless of the city or country, it is essential to have a good sampling before drawing conclusions. Since before meeting me, some people already shared my opinion about the proper name for the Castilian language, some have used the two names as synonyms, but after hearing my explanations began calling it **Castilian** exclusively, and a third group suffers from apathy about this important issue.

5

WHY THE LANGUAGE MANY CALL "SPANISH" MUST BE CALLED CASTILIAN

Just like the other examples shown earlier in this book, Castilian is another language that pre-existed the country where it is now the primary official language (together with other languages that — according to the Spanish Constitution— are also official in their respective regions). It is both imprecise and pejorative to call Castilian "Spanish". It would be absurd to call the English language "UK-ish" or "UnitedKingdomish". In the United Kingdom, the speakers of Cornish (*Kernowek* or *Kernewek*), Gaelic, Irish (Irish Gaelic, a Goidelic language), Scots, or Welsh (*Cymraeg* or *Gymraeg*) would certainly object if the King or Queen tried to impose that name to the English language, when several different languages are spoken natively.

During the era of the Soviet Union, it would have been absurd if a Russian said: "I speak Soviet". It would also be incorrect to say that the official language of Israel is "Israeli" or that the official language of Iran is "Iranian". The official language of Israel is called Hebrew. The official language of Iran is Farsi (aka Persian). The point is that in all of these countries (Iran, Israel, the the United Kingdom), the official language existed way before the current political structure did, and that's why the language nomenclature in these countries doesn't match the country name.

After Franco's death, the new Spanish Constitution of 1978 fortunately corrected the linguicide attempt and its Article 3 states:

> Castilian is the official language of the State. All Spaniards have the obligation to know it, and the right to use it.
>
> The other Spanish languages shall also be official in their respective autonomous communities, according to their statutes.
>
> The richness of Spain's diverse linguistic modalities represents our national heritage and shall be the object of special respect and protection.

In addition, the Constitutions of several countries in the Americas —including Bolivia, Colombia, Ecuador, El Salvador, Paraguay, Perú, and Venezuela— also state that the official language is Castilian (together with other languages in some cases). In most schools in Venezuela, report cards state that the class is called *"Castellano y literatura"* (Castilian and Literature). Although the Mexican Constitution doesn't currently indicate any official language, the former President Vicente Fox stated:

> *"Con el castellano podemos atravesar veinte fronteras sin que perdamos comunicación...".*

or:

> "With Castilian, we can cross 20 international borders without losing the message..."

In the upcoming chapter, we'll talk more about what he stated in his inauguration speech at the Language Congress in Valladolid.

6

VICENTE FOX AT THE LANGUAGE CONGRESS IN VALLADOLID

During his inauguration speech at the Language Congress in Valladalid, former Mexican President Vicente Fox gave a breathtaking presentation. In the Castilan version of this book (*La conspiración del castellano*), I covered it completely. For this English version of the book, I am only going to cover two excerpts. Here's the first:

"... La lengua no sólo nos permite la comunicación sino que configura nuestro pensamiento, nuestra sensibilidad, nuestra visión del mundo. La lengua de algún modo nos crea, nos conforma, nos define".

Or, in English:

"... Language doesn't only allow us to communicate, but it

also configures our thought process, our sensitivity, and our vision of the world. One way or another, language creates us and defines us."

These words from Vicente Fox underline the ones I wrote in the introduction of this book: *Words make worlds*. The inappropriate use of the term "Spanish" instead—or as a synonym for— "Castilian" causes a misconfiguration in the human thought process. First, non-Castilian speakers who hear the term "Spanish" will imagine (incorrectly) that there is a single native language spoken in Spain. Second, Catalonians or Basques can feel uncomfortable in their own country of Spain, since calling Castilian "Spanish" marginalizes their own language and culture. On the other hand, when we call Castilian by its proper name, we are underlining the fact that Castilian, Euskera/Basque, Galician and Valencian are Spanish languages (plural), just as the Spanish Constitution of 1978 states, as we quoted it in the prior chapter of this book.

Here's the second excerpt from Vicente Fox:

"Con el castellano podemos atravesar veinte fronteras sin que perdamos comunicación; sólo hacemos, en esos casos, más amplio el espectro de nuestro vocabulario ante la emergencia de las voces locales, que suelen causar más simpatía que desencuentro".

Or, in English:

"With Castilian, we can cross 20 international borders without losing the message; by doing so, we only make the spectrum of our vocabulary grow as we are suddenly exposed to local regionalisms which cause more pleasantness than disappointment."

I'll cover the effect of Castilian regionalisms ahead in this book, but first some essential information about the language's caretaker.

THE FIRST CASTILIAN GRAMMAR BOOK

The first Castilian grammar book (*Gramática castellana*) was written by Antonio de Nebrija and published in 1492. As far as we know, it was the first work about the Castilian language and its rules. Antonio's more complete name is **Elio Antonio Martínez de Cala y Xarana**, although he is better known as **Elio Antonio de Nebrija, de Nebrixa** or **de Lebrija**. He was born in the palindromic year of 1441 and died in 1522.

8

THE ROYAL SPANISH ACADEMY AND THE VATICAN

The Royal Spanish Academy (*Real Academia Española*) was founded in 1713. The title of its first Dictionary was *Diccionario de la lengua castellana compuesto por la Real Academia Española* or translated to English: "Dictionary of the Castilian Language composed by the Royal Spanish Academy".

Ahead you'll see its cover.

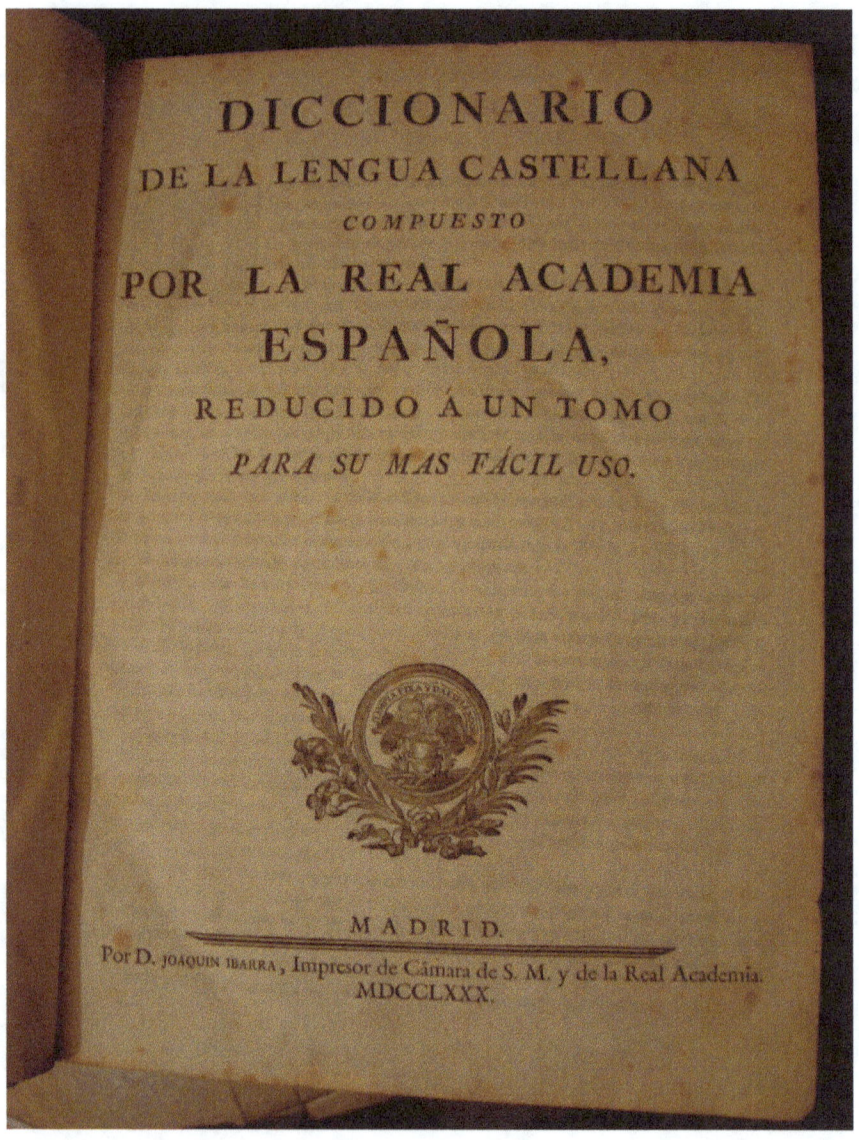

The name of this dictionary has the same proper name for the language as does the first Castilian grammar book of 1492, which we covered in the prior chapter. From 1780 until 1925, the Academy maintained the same proper (Castilian)

name in its title. The first contaminated version came with the 1925 edition, which sadly was changed to be called *Diccionario de la lengua española*.

Let's do the math: Between 1492 (the year of the first Castilian grammar book) and 1925 (the year of the Royal Academy's treason), we had 433 years of consistency in the language's proper name.

Just as the Royal Spanish Academy committed a crime against humanity in 1925, the Vatican committed a similar one in 1632, when Galileo published his *Dialogue Concerning the Two Chief World Systems*, where he defended the Copernican system as opposed to the traditional Ptolemaic one, where the latter states that the Sun revolves around the Earth. As a direct result, the Vatican condemned Galileo for heresy.

Fortunately, in 1992, Pope John Paul II —359 years after the sentence— rectified Galileo's inappropriate condemnation while he simultaneously presented the 1820 book *Copernico, Galileo e la Chiesa. Fine della controversia* (*End of the controversy*, 1820), which clarifies that stating that the Earth revolves around the sun is not a blasphemy.

Just as Pope John Paul II recognized that crime of the Vatican and rectified it, soon we'll see the director of the Royal Spanish Academy do the same, by reestablishing the proper name of the official Dictionary. Hopefully, the director will do it in a parallel way to what did the Pope did, by simultaneously presenting this same book, *The Castilian Conspiracy* or its original version *La conspiración del castellano*.

In the meantime, Javier Llorente, computer programmer and creator of an Android app that directly accesses the Royal Academy's Dictionary, got a head start when creating the app, since he appropriately named it *Diccionario castellano de la Real Academia Española*. Here is the screenshot:

This is stupendous! Although I don't know him personally yet, ¡*gracias Javier*!

Observation from the second edition: This app has sadly been removed from the Android PlayStore, but it's still in my current Android and is available for the asking.

9
ANDRÉS BELLO'S GRAMMAR BOOK

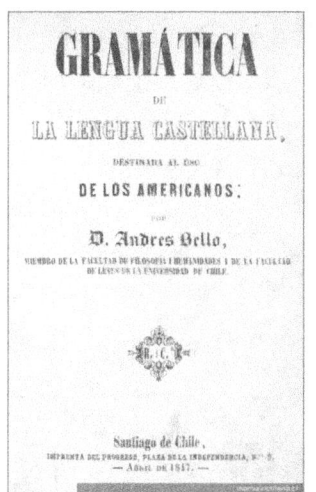

I adore the work of Andrés Bello (1781 — 1865), who was a Venezuelan who was later nationalized as a Chilean. I love the title, *Gramática de la lengua castellana destinada al uso de los americanos*, (*Grammar of the Castilian language focused on the Americans*), because it properly calls both the language and the habitants of the zone. America is the name of a continent, not a particular country. That's why the OAS (Organization of American States) is called that way. Chile and Venezuela were among the 21 founding countries of the OAS, as was my country, the United States.

10
THE CHILEAN LAW THAT PROTECTS CASTILIAN

The Chilean law called The Constitutional Organic Law of Teaching (*Ley Orgánica Constitucional de Enseñanza*, N° 18.962) by the Ministry of Education, published on March 10, 1990, indicates in its Article ii that:

First, here's the original in Castilian:

"Los alumnos de la enseñanza básica deberán alcanzar los siguientes requisitos mínimos de egreso: punto a) Saber leer y escribir; expresarse correctamente en el idioma castellano en forma oral y escrita, y ser capaz de apreciar otros modos de comunicación."

This translates to:

"Students in basic education must meet the following minimum graduation requirements: point a) Know how to read and write; Express yourself correctly in the Castilian language in oral and written form, and be able to appreciate other modes of communication."

Bravo to the Chilean legislators who used the proper name for the Castilian language!

11

CASTILIAN AND THE DRUM

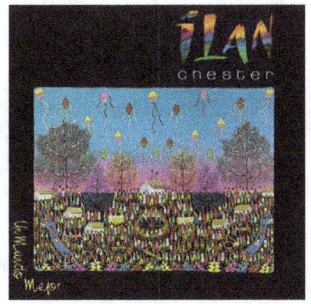

Venezuelan singer Ilan Chester (born in Israel as Ilan Czenstochouski), is one of my favorites. Even though I'm not Hispanic, I'm very familiar and love several of Ilan's songs, but one of my absolute favorites is **El castellano y el tambor** (which translates as **Castilian and the drum**), from the album *Un mundo mejor* (*A better world*).

. . .

Thanks Ilan by creating a better world (in part) by calling the Castilian language properly!

12

MYTHS ABOUT THE TERMS CASTELLANO AND CASTILIAN

There are people who incorrectly state that Castilian (or *castellano*) is the version of the language spoken in some regions of Spain, where the letters **c** and **z** are pronounced differently from the **s**. This is an unfortunate myth. The name of the language is Castilian (*castellano*) whether or not the **c** and **z** are pronounced with their unique sound (similar to the **th** sound in English) or with the **s** sound, which is generally the case in the Americas, some parts of Andalusia (which is spelled as *Andalucía* in Castilian), and in the Canary Islands.

There are differences between Australian English, Bahamian English, Canadian English, and US English. There are even regional differences between Boston English, Georgia English, or New York English, but they are all still English, just as there are differences between Argentinian ("Argentine") Castilian, Chilean Castilian, Colombian Castilian,

Cuban Castilian, Mexican Castilian, Puerto Rican Castilian, and Venezuelan Castilian. However, it's always Castilian.

There are also people who affirm that we should only use the Castilian term for old literature like *Cantar del mío Cid*, but not for what we speak today. That is as silly as saying that what Shakespeare wrote was English, but we speak today is not. What we speak today is modern Castilian and modern English.

13
WHERE CASTILIAN IS SPOKEN TODAY

Here is a list of places where Castilian is spoken today as a primary or secondary language (It may be incomplete.):

- Andorra (second language. The primary one is Catalán.)
- Argentina
- Bolivia
- Chile
- Colombia
- Costa Rica
- Cuba
- Dominican Republic
- Ecuador
- Equatorial Guinea
- El Salvador
- Guatemala

- Honduras
- México
- Nicaragua
- Panamá
- Perú
- Paraguay
- Puerto Rico
- Spain
- United States (Second language)
- Uruguay
- Venezuela

14

WHEN IT IS CORRECT AND APPROPRIATE TO SAY "SPANISH"

It is appropriate to use the term **Spanish** as an adjective when describing things related to Spain, as in the following examples:

- Castilian is the most widely used **Spanish** language. Catalán, Euskera (Basque), Galician and Valencian are also important **Spanish** languages in their particular regions.
- I often quote the **Spanish** Constitution.
- **Spanish** dance, **Spanish** food, and **Spanish** wine are known throughout the world.

As you'll have noted, when **Spanish** properly refers to languages, it does so in a plural way, just like when we speak about African languages, Asian languages, or European languages.

15

FAQ ABOUT CASTILIAN

Why is the language called Castilian?

Castilian is called that way because it originated in Castile (*Castilla*) (which is now part of the Kingdom of Spain), just as English is called English because it originated in England (which is now part of the United Kingdom). Spain is really a group of independent countries which were unified, just as the United Kingdom is a group of countries that did the same.

I have a friend who is from (one of those countries where they speak Castilian as the primary language), and s/he always said that her/his language is "Spanish". Why?

Your friend was being imprecise, either out of convenience or out of ignorance. Whatever the reason, the fact that s/he called the language "Spanish" proves that part of Franco's mission is still partially successful decades after his death and after the correction/consolation in the Spanish Constitution of 1978 (which we quoted earlier in this book)... but now that you and I both know the truth, it's our responsibility to fix that. Very educated Castilian speakers know the truth about this, although some of them imprecisely refer to the Castilian language as "Spanish" ("*español*") either because they think you won't understand (and don't want to invest the time into educating you about it) or they suffer from "third-party guilt" and would prefer to bury the issue than to illuminate it. The time has come to correct this situation once and for all! We must end the cover-up now: not tomorrow, but today!

16

MINAM: MYTH REGARDING ACCENTUATION OF UPPERCASE LETTERS

I'd have lots of money if I had a dollar or euro for every person who as falsely stated that you must never accentuate upper case letters in Castilian. So much is the case that over a decade ago, I created an acronym to describe the phenomenon: MINAM (*Mito de la no acentuación de las mayúsculas*, or Myth about accentuation of uppercase letters). Beyond simple logic (since accent marks help us determine the pronunciation, especially with unknown words or names in Castilian), The Royal Academy clearly states that the rules of accentuation apply equally to upper case letters as to lowercase ones, and that the Academy has never changed this in its entire history.

I believe the myth was born because many mechanical typewriters couldn't accentuate upper case letters, so an "unofficial exemption" spread like wildfire. When combined with laziness, some people to this day still write in all caps because the pseudo immunity.

Over 15 years ago, when my now deceased colleague Alexis Márquez Rodríguez (author of the book *Con la lengua* or *With the tongue*) received a related question about accentuation of upper case letters in his column in the Venezuelan newspaper *El Nacional*, he properly answered by affirming the logic and the rules, while he commented about the tech challenge that existed with mechanical typewriters and some computers (of that era). From my Florida office, I became aware of his column and I immediately overnighted him an envelope with the solution on a diskette, together with several of my articles. The following week, I had the happy surprise of receiving a phone call from my friend, the Venezuelan writer Cristina Policastro, who confirmed that Alexis Márquez Rodríguez had dedicated his next column to the tech solutions I had sent to him, and to quote some of my articles about the proper Castilianization of foreign tech terms (which we'll cover ahead in this book).

17

CASTILIAN KEYBOARD OR SPANISH KEYBOARD?

Is it correct to say Castilian keyboard or Spanish keyboard? It depends:

Generally speaking, *physical* keyboards are classified by region, not by language*. As a result, there are no *physical* English keyboards or *physical* Castilian keyboards, anywhere in the world. Instead, there are physical Australian, Canadian, US, and UK keyboards, just as there are Latin American** and Spanish keyboards.

On the other hand, *virtual* keyboards —the ones we find on our smartphones (Android and iPhone) and tablets (Android and iPad) are indeed classified by language, although they usually have a similar layout to their respective region, at least as they come from the factory.

*There are a few exceptions with the physical keyboard rule, like the Swiss German or French Canadian physical keyboards.

**If you are among those who reject the term "Latin American", I want to clarify that the Latin American keyboard classification wasn't created by me, but by the manufacturers. Ahead in this book, I'll defend the essential use of the the term "Latin American" in certain situations.

In the next chapter, we'll see the superiority of the Spanish (ISO) keyboard.

18

THE SUPERIORITY OF THE SPANISH KEYBOARD

The physical Spanish keyboard (both the Spanish ISO keyboards from Apple and other manufacturers and non-ISO Spanish versions from other manufacturers) have many advantages over the Latin American keyboard (which Apple used to simply call "Spanish" before Apple switched to the ISO version, and other manufacturers still call "Latin American"). It is not a question of patriotism, but of practical facts in their design and use.

- The Spanish (ISO) keyboard fortunately has the @ symbol on the **2** key (just like the US keyboard). This is advantageous for people who frequently migrate between different computers, one of which has a US keyboard. On the other hand, the Latin American keyboard has the @ symbol on the letter **Q**.
- The Spanish (ISO) keyboard fortunately has the ascending accent used in Castilian in the middle

row next to the **Ñ**, which is very ergonomic. On the other hand, the Latin American keyboard has the Castilian accent mark next to the letter **P**, which means that every time you have to accent a letter, you must raise your pinky, which promotes carpal tunnel syndrome.

- The Spanish (ISO) keyboard has the necessary symbols to type both masculine (i.e. 1º, 2º, 3º) and feminine ordinal numbers (1ª, 2ª, 3ª). This symbol with the underlined **a** in superscript (in some fonts) is also used to abbreviate the name **María**, especially when used with a middle name, as in the cases of **Mª Cristina**, **Mª Luisa**, and others. Unfortunately the Latin American keyboard is *machista* (chauvinistic), since it lacks the feminine symbol.
- The Spanish (ISO) keyboard includes both the € for the euro and the $ which is used for both dollars and pesos. The Latin American keyboard unfortunately lacks the euro symbol.
- The Spanish (ISO) keyboard also includes everything to write directly in many languages including Castilian, Catalán, Galician, English, French, Portuguese, and Italian.

With the Spanish (ISO) keyboard, the standard QWERTY layout is maintained. Only a few symbols change position and —compared with the US keyboard— it has additional keys. In fact, since it can handle so many languages and currencies directly, in my opinion the Spanish ISO should replace several existing physical keyboards, including both

Canadian, the French, Latin American, Italian, and US. The end user will get a better product and the manufacturers will simplify their production, thus reducing cost.

I applaud Apple, BTC, and Logitech for offering the Spanish ISO keyboard in the Americas (instead of the Latin American keyboard) and I recommend other manufacturers like Dell, HP, Lenovo, and Sony do the same, for their benefit and that of their users in the Americas.

Differences between the Spanish ISO and the non-ISO:

There are two types of physical Spanish keyboards (excluding Latin American keyboards), both the ISO and non-ISO. (I am excluding the very old so-called "Spanish" keyboard Apple stopped selling in the 1990s, which really had a Latin American layout.) The only difference between is that the non-ISO physical Spanish keyboards are missing the dedicated greater (>) and greater (<) keys. When using a non-ISO Spanish keyboard, to access these symbols, it's necessary a modifier key with the Z key or the same modifier key together with the Shift key and the Z key.

19
FAULTY LANGUAGE, DEFECTIVE THOUGHT PROCESS

In the mid 1990s, the *Universidad del Sagrado Corazón* (University of the Sacred Heart) in Puerto Rico created a series of public service announcements to combat Castinglish (commonly but inaccurately known as "Spanglish") called *Idioma defectuoso, pensamiento defectuoso* (Faulty language, defective thought process). They are narrated by well known public figures from the *isla del encanto* (Enchanted Island). Here is the text of from one of them (followed by an adaptation in English):

El idioma es la sangre del espíritu.

Háblalo bien... con orgullo.

No digas *nice*.

Di **chévere** o **tremendo**.

No digas *size*.

Di **talla** o **tamaño**.

Tampoco digas: "Estoy en *shock*".

Es mejor decir: "Estoy **atónito** o **perplejo**"

Brown es incorrecto. Usa **marrón**, **castaño** o **pardo**.

Tuna es la que canta. En español (sic), se come **atún**.

Idioma defectuoso, pensamiento defectuoso.

Mensaje de la Universidad del Sagrado Corazón y de esta emisora.

Or in English (for clarification only):

Language is the blood of the spirit.

Speak it well… with pride.

Don't say **nice**.

Say *chévere* or *tremendo*.

Don't say *size*.

Say *talla* or *tamaño*.

Don't say "I'm in **shock**".

It's better to say: "I am *atónito* or *perplejo*"

Brown is incorrect. Use *marrón, castaño* o *pardo*.

Tuna is the one that sings. In Spanish (sic), we eat *atún*.

Faulty language, defective thought process.

Message from the University of the Sacred Heart and this station.

I applaud everyone involved with this project, including the camera operators, editors, presenters, producers, and writers. I just they had used the appropriate name for the Castilian language.

In the next chapter, we'll cover healthy Castilianization versus Castenglish.

20

HEALTHY CASTILIANIZATION VERSUS CASTENGLISH

I offer infinite thanks to my friend and godfather of the first words I Castilianized over fifteen years ago. Ríchard Izarra, founder of PRODU.com and director of the Izarra editorial group, accepted the use of the Castilianized words I had created (my first "daughters" so far, since the word *palabras* is feminine in Castilian) and published the following article where I presented them to the world.

The Castilian códec

Although the word **códec** (which comes from the words **encode** and **decode**) is primarily used in the audio and video worlds, I have extended the term to linguistics. A códec is an algorithm (or device) to convert an audible or visual signal into a recordable one. The Castilian códec is an algorithm to convert the sound of words into written words. Unlike other languages like English and French, the Castilian códec guarantees us a consistent sound system, so if I write some words down on a piece of paper, whether they are simple or complex, any Castilian-speaking person on the other side of the world will be able to read them aloud with nearly perfect fidelity, despite the fact that they may be unknown to the reader, almost as if the paper were an audio recorder. This consistent sound system is not only a practical advantage, it represents a Castilian *cultural heritage*. Here you'll see some words and how they were properly Castilianized in order to comply with the Castilian códec.

Foreign word	Castilianized word, singular	Castilianized word, plural
tunnel	el túnel	los túneles
train	el tren	los trenes
sweater	el suéter	los suéteres
polyester	el poliéster	los poliésteres
leader	el líder	los líderes
homerun	el jonrón	los jonrones

The last one —*jonrón*— is the most recent. Even though the word *jonrón* has been used in newspapers for many years, the Royal Academy only admitted it very recently in the twenty-third edition of its Dictionary.

The true role of dictionaries

Some people mistakenly believe that dictionaries exist to restrict the creation of new words. That is inaccurate. Dictionaries exist to document the accepted spellings and meanings of words that already exist, in order to have consistency with them. That's why dictionaries habitually come out with new editions that include new words. Other people mistakenly believe that they must wait until a new word appears in the dictionary before using it. That is not true either. With very few exceptions, new words are born in use and are later recognized and documented (admitted) by dictionaries. The only quite exceptional case I know was when a Castilian word was accepted into the Royal Academy before being in popular use was when the Venezuelan ex-President Caldera requested the Academy to add the word *millardo*, a synonym of *mil millones* or thousand million, commonly expressed in the United States as "billion", which has absolutely no relationship to do with the amount in Castilian's *billón*. *Billón* in Castilian has 12 zeros, while **billion** in US English (and UK English since 1974) has only 9 zeros.

Some words that will always be treated as foreign

Of course, we don't have any obligation to Castilianize all of the foreign words we need or want to use. For example, terms like *déjà vu* we maintain as foreign due to their nature. In those cases, in order to protect our sacred Castilian códec, we write them in italics.

Decision, with the corresponding message

A few years ago, my friend Rubén Abruña (of EditTraining.com) and I had to convince an important pro video system manufacturer to accept the words *sóftwer* and *járdwer* (which I had Castilianized over fifteen years earlier) in their printed materials. Rubén and I were collaborating on the translation/localization of those materials. When we saw their initial resistance, I created the following presentation so they would understand the profound ramifications of their three possible options.

Decision	Sentence	Associated message
Castilianize	XXXX es un sóftwer líder en la edición de video.	"I have accepted these words with all rights and privileges, just like a naturalized citizen in my country".
Treat as foreign terms in italics	XXXX es un *software leader* en la edición de video.	"I use these words, but I consider them to be foreign and distant. That's why I write them in italics."
End of the sacred Castilian phonetic system	XXXX es un software leader en la edición de video.	"Screw the cultural heritage. I don't give a damn that for centuries we have respected the Castilian phonetic system. I don't care if my son or granddaughter is embarriased because she mispronounces the words and is ridiculed".

Decision: Sentence

Foreign word	Castilianized word
tunnel	el túnel
train	el tren
sweater	el suéter
polyester	el poliéster
leader	el líder
homerun	el jonrón
software	el sóftwer
hardware	el járdwer

(Actually, the presentation we gave them was audio-visual, so they could hear how people could mispronounce the words if they chosen option three.)

Of course, the moral of the story (just like all of the other words that have been Castilianized in the past) is simple: It's our responsibility to maintain the sacred Castilian códec. Even though they may look strange at first, this was not the first nor the last time that something like that has happened, or will happen. Certainly our (Castilian-speaking) grandparents found the words *túnel*, *tren*, *suéter*, *poliéster*, and *líder* strange at first, they got used to them in order to protect the sacred Castilian códec and the cultural heritage.

Foreign word	Castilianized word
tunnel	el túnel
train	el tren
sweater	el suéter
polyester	el poliéster
leader	el líder
homerun	el jonrón
software	el sóftwer
hardware	el járdwer

So our new Castilianized words like *sóftwer* and *járdwer* must join the others.

Related stats

I Castilianized *sóftwer* over fifteen years ago.

At publication time of this book, Google showed 25,300 results after doing a search for *sóftwer*, and the number increases continually.

21

WHY THE WORD INTERNET MUST TREATED AS FEMININE

The word **Internet** in Castilian must be treated as feminine because the name of a network, which in Castilian is the feminine word *red*. Every time people say *la Internet*, in their mind, it is understood that they are saying *la red Internet*, but they are just skipping that word. It's the same when they refer to a highway like *la Palmetto*, a known one in the Miami area. It is understood that in their mind they are saying *la autopista Palmetto*.

Just as in English, when they refer to the public Internet, in Castilian the noun should be written with an uppercase **I**. (There is a seldom-used instance of **internet** with a lower case in both English and Castilian to refer to a private internal network, like an intranet. In that seldom-used case, it must be written in lower case both in English and in Castilian.)

The reason to write the public Internet with an initial upper case I is because it is treated with the same rule as for a sovereign nation, which are also written with an initial upper case letter. However, just as demonyms and nationalities must be written with their initial letter in lowercase in Castilian (the opposite of the English rule), the adjectives for the Internet (*internética, internético,* two of my "daughters") must be written with an initial lower case, unless the initiate a sentence, or –due to a style— are written in a title in all caps. Some examples of that would be:

- *El servicio internético en mi casa es muy rápido.*
- *La conexión internética es muy lenta en algunos hoteles.*

22

WHAT THE MARKET DEMANDS IS...

As I have indicated previously, I applaud the properly made and justifiable Castilianizations, but I reject those which are damaging. Sadly, some people have chosen to Castilianize the English word **marketing** as *márketing* (with an accent mark) or *marketing* (without any accent mark): That is damaging because it interrupts the direct comprehension of the the fundamental relationship between *el mercado* (**the market**), *el mercadeo* (marketing) and the verb *mercadear* (**to market**). If you are among those who have been using *márketing* in Castilian, are you really willing to Castilianize **el** *márket* too? I hope not!

23

THE DANGER OF ENGLISH-LANGUAGE SOFTWARE FOR CASTILIAN-SPEAKERS

Below you'll see an updated version of an article I published in 1995 in *Producción & Distribución* magazine. The article explains how Castilian-speakers who are only exposed to English-language software end up speaking Castenglish, and are denied the knowledge of knowing the words that exist and are available in Castilian in most cases. First you'll see the Castilian version of the article, followed by an adaptation for those who only read English.

La amenaza del sóftwer en inglés

Éste es un aviso importante: A continuación hemos impreso unas cuantas palabras fuertes que podrían ser ofensivas para algunos de nuestros lectores. Si eres sensible a las palabras fuertes, no sigas leyendo. He aquí algunas frases comúnmente oídas entre usuarios castellanhablantes de computadoras:

"¿Ya *printeaste* el documento? No, es que mi *printer* está dañado. ¿Salvaste tu trabajo en el *hard disk*? ¿Hiciste el *backup*? No, primero tengo que *cuitear* el programa que estoy usando. ¿Dónde está tu *mouse*? ¿Cuánto mide ese *file*? ¿Lo hiciste en un *database* o un *word processor*? ¡Mándamelo por el *network*!"

Es una lástima que algunos programas aún no hayan salido en castellano. Pero la mayoría de los programas populares sí están disponibles y lo que duele más es que tantas personas que se sienten más cómodas hablando en castellano (y tampoco quieren estudiar otro idioma) compren (o se les ofrezca únicamente) sóftwer en inglés, aun cuando existen versiones en su idioma. En muchas academias de la informática en países castellanoamericanos se emplea puro sóftwer, textos y hasta teclados enfocados en el idioma inglés. La informática no debería ser un lujo reservado para los anglohablantes ni debería ser la causa de la deformación del castellano.

En los ejemplos citados en el segundo párrafo, existen dos fenómenos lingüísticos que merecen señalarse: la castellanización y los calcos innecesarios de términos que tienen perfectas traducciones. Al usar u obligar el uso de sóftwer en inglés, se le niega el conocimiento de la computación a los castellanohablantes en su propio idioma y termina obligándoles a hablar como en nuestros ejemplos. Todos deben tener el derecho a saber que existen los términos **impresora, imprimir, copia de respaldo, salir, ratón, archivo, base de datos, procesador de textos** y **red**.

En la lingüística, el término **calco** se refiere a la práctica de aplicar un significado extranjero y nuevo a una palabra ya existente. Decir "salvar" en lugar de **guardar** es aplicar el significado del verbo *to save*, que es más amplio en inglés que en castellano. En inglés, *to save* abarca tanto las connotaciones **rescatar** y **almacenar**. En castellano, **salvar** sólo abarca la idea de **rescatar**. Este fenómeno ocurre a menudo en el sur de la Florida con palabras ajenas a la informática, por ejemplo **venta** por **oferta, rebaja** o **liquidación**... aplicar por **solicitar**... llamar para atrás por **devolver la llamada**... y **correr para presidente** por **postularse para la presidencia**. Estos calcos causan bastante confusión para los castellanohablantes recién llegados a los Estados Unidos y están tan integrados en el lenguaje aquí como muchas palabras italianas en el lunfardo de Buenos Aires, Argentina. Hasta conocemos el caso de una señora venezolana que salió tristemente de una mueblería del sur de la Florida porque el vendedor le dijo que su sofá favorito no estaba "en venta". El vendedor quiso decir que no estaba "en oferta" y a pesar de las serias intenciones de la señora de comprarlo a cualquier precio, ambos perdieron debido a la falta de comunicación. Por otro lado, existen cuñas en la radio local que dicen que en X tienda "Toda la ropa está en venta..." y se preguntan si la semana pasada sólo la alquilaban. ¡En serio!

Negar el conocimiento de los términos nativos de la computación a los castellanohablantes es tan grave como enseñarles que no deben acentuarse las mayúsculas, aun cuando la lógica, la Real Academia Española y todas las gramáticas dicen lo contrario. Una de las características más adoradas del castellano es que éste nos garantiza poder pronunciar correctamente cualquier palabra, aunque ésta sea desconocida. Si no seguimos la regla de la acentuación de las mayúsculas, perderemos esta valiosa característica y seguirán ocurriendo contratiempos como cuando llegué a Venezuela la primera vez y leí "Avila" y no **Ávila**. Por fortuna, ¡American Airlines ahora acentúa la **A** en **Los Ángeles** y los últimos BOLÍVARES venezolanos tienen la **I** mayúscula tildada! Sólo falta que el gobierno colombiano acentúe la "U" en "REPÚBLICA" en los pasaportes.

Hablando de American Airlines, al parecer les encanta el calco "Damas y caballeros, el capitán..." (como si estuvieran presentando un espectáculo) en lugar del legítimo "Señores pasajeros..."

Negar un teclado español a los castellanohablantes les obliga a recordar rebuscadas combinaciones de teclas, lo que en muchos casos causa que vayan por el camino de menor resistencia, que es escribir sin eñes, acentos ortográficos (tildes), diéresis y otros caracteres. El supuesto pretexto de escribir todo en mayúsculas tampoco es un defensa válida.

No dejemos que nos gane la amenaza del sóftwer en

inglés. Como bien dice una nota para el usuario de Microsoft, "... compartimos la misma lengua y todos tenemos que sentirnos orgullosos y responsables de ella".

Here is the adapted version for English-only readers:

The danger of English-language software

for Castilian-speakers

This is an important warning: Ahead you will see some strong and alarming words which may be sensitive to some readers. If you are very sensitive to strong words, don't continue reading. Here are some common sentences shared among Castilian-speakers who are only exposed to English-language software:

"¿Ya printeaste el documento? (Did you already print the document?)

No, es que mi printer está dañado. (No, my printer is broken.)

¿Salvaste tu trabajo en el hard disk? (Did you save your work on the hard disk?)

¿Hiciste el backup? (Did you do the backup?)

No, primero tengo que cuitear el programa que estoy usando. (No, first I have to Quit the program I am using.)

¿Dónde está tu mouse? (Where is your mouse?)

¿Cuánto mide ese file? (How much does that file weigh?)

¿Lo hiciste en un *database* o un *word processor*? (Did you create it in a database or in a word processor?)

¡Mándamelo por el network!" (Sent it to me through the network!)

It is a shame that a few programs are not yet available in Castilan, but the majority of popular software is indeed already available, and what hurts even more is that so many people who are more comfortable communicating in Castilian (and have no desire to study another language) buy (or are only offered) software in English, even when there are versions available in their preferred language. Sadly, in many institutes in Castilian America, only English software and US keyboards are used. Computing should not be a luxury reserved only for English-speakers, nor it should be the cause of the deformation of the Castilian language.

In the examples quoted in the second paragraph, there are two different linguistic phenomena that need to be pointed out: Castilianization and unnecessary calques (calques are words or phrases borrowed from another language by literal, word-for-word or root-for-root translation) of terms that have perfect and standardized translations in Castilian. By forcing the use of English-language software, decision-makers are denying computing knowledge in the Castilian-speakers' own language, and leaves them no choice but to speak as in our examples at the beginning of this article. All Castilian-speakers should have the right to know that there are terms in their language like *impresora, imprimir, copia de respaldo, salir, ratón, archivo, base de datos, procesador de textos,* and *red.*

To say *"salvar"* instead of the legitimate *guardar* is to calque the verb **to save**, which is broader in English than in Castilian, since in English, it covers both "storing" and "rescuing", but *salvar* only applies to "rescuing", which is not appropriate.

The phenomenon is frequently visible in South Florida with works beyond computing, like when some people say *venta* in cases when they should be saying *oferta, rebaja* o *liquidación... aplicar* in cases where they really meant to say *solicitar... llamar para atrás* when they really should use *devolver la llamada,* and *correr para la presidencia* instead of *postularse para la presidencia.* These calques are so integrated into the language here as Italian words are in the Lunfardo dialect of Buenos Aires, Argentina, and they cause great confusion for recent arrivals. I even know the case of a Venezuelan woman who sadly left a furniture store in Miami because the salesman told her that the couch she wanted to buy was not *"en venta"* ("for sale"). What the salesman really should have sent that it was not "en oferta" ("on sale" or "on special"). Despite the woman's serious intentions to buy it at any price, both lost due to the lack of communication. On the radio, we hear commercials that say that *"Toda la ropa está en venta..."* ("All of the clothing is for sale...") and new arrivals ask themselves whether the prior week they only rented the clothes there. Seriously!

Denying the knowledge of native computing terms is as bad as teaching students that they must not (or are not required to) accentuate upper case letters when both logic and the Royal Academy's rules say that they must. One of the most coveted features of the Castilian language is the guarantee that any word (even unknown ones) can be pronounced correctly. If people don't follow the rule about accentuating upper case letters, they will lose that valuable feature, and mishaps will continuing to occur, like when I went to Venezuela the first time and read alond *"Avila"* and not *Ávila*. Fortunately, American Airlines now accentuates the **A** in **Los Ángeles** and the most recent Venezuelan **BOLÍVARES** have the upper case **I** accentuated! Now we only need the Colombian government to accent the **U** in *REPÚBLICA* in their passports.

Speaking of American Airlines, apparently they love the calque "Damas y caballeros, el capitán..." ("Ladies and gentlemen, the Captain..."), as if they were about to start a show, rather than the standardized airline expression *"Señores pasajeros..."*

To deny a Spanish keyboard to Castilian speakers forces them to recall and apply awkward key combinations, which in many cases, makes them follow to the path of least resistance: to write without the ñ/Ñ character, accent marks, umlaut (often used of the letter **ü** in words like **Camagüey, Mayagüez,** *nicaragüense,* and *vergüenza*), the ordinal numbers (both feminine and masculine) and other characters. The supposed excuse of writing in all upper case is not valid.

Let us not allow English-language software damage the Castilian-language or the user experience for Castilian speakers. As a Microsoft user manual says, "...We all share the same language and we must all feel proud and responsible for it".

24

SAY IT IN CASTILIAN, SAY IT PROUDLY

In 2008 in Venezuela, the phone company known as CANTV created a pro-Castilian campaign in all of its offices nationwide. The campaign was called *Dilo en castellano, dilo con orgullo (***Say it in Castilian, say it proudly***)*. Its primary objective was to make people aware about the good use of the Castilian language as an indispensable social practice to maintain the culture alive in the country. According to CANTV, the campaign was born out of the concern from their General Management and Public Relations departments, since they saw that telecommunications jargon was unnecessarily being based upon anglo sources and that by using them so much, the were being treated as if they were true Castilian terms.

The text on the left says: "We approach, understand, and feel the world in Castilian. In the new CANTV, we speak Castilian with Venezuelan pride."

I applaud CANTV's initiative, and of course, their use of the proper name Castilian (*castellano*) at all times.

25

THE CASTILIAN ALPHABET AND ITS PAINS

Currently the Castilian alphabet contains 27 letters, although up until 1994, it had 29. In 1994, the letters **ch** and **ll** were eliminated from the Castilian alphabet, but the sounds produced by these two letters remain. The **ch** sound is pronounced the same as in English, while in modern Castilian, the **ll** is pronounced most popularly as a **y**. (i.e. most pronounce the last name *Castillo* as if it were spelled "Castiyo".). There is still a small number of people who pronounce the Castilian *ll* sound as an **ly**, i.e. "Castilyo". Even though the **ch** and **ll** are no longer letters in the Castilian alphabet, they are still inseparable when writing them. For example, if you are writing a letter or book and you run out of space at the end of a line, when performing hyphenation in Castilian (or with proper Castilian names in other languages), the two letters must stay together. The two pairs of letters were eliminated from the alphabet in order to standardize the way to handle alphabetization. With the older system, a list of words in Castilian had to be put into alphabetical order like this:

- carro
- coche
- curso
- chino
- domicilio
- lámpara
- luz
- lluvia

With the new system, it's like this (just like in English):

- carro
- chino
- coche
- curso
- domicilio
- lámpara
- lluvia
- luz

I am in complete agreement with this change. Now the Castilian language contains the following letters: **a, b, c, d, e, f, g, h, i, j, k, l, m, n, ñ, o, p, q, r, s, t, u, v, w, x, y,** and **z**. The letters **k** and **w** exist in the language primarily for Castilianized words like *kilo*, *sóftwer*, *járdwer*, and *web*, as we covered earlier in this book.

Four of these letters are problematic, because their names vary from country to country. The problematic letters are **b, v, w,** and **y**. Unlike regional uses of words (which we'll cover ahead in this book), I believe that there must be a global unification of the names of these letters (or at least three of them), just as the Royal Academy suggests in its *Ortografía de la lengua española* (sic) (2010). The only difference between the Academy's position and mine is that theirs states that the other names are not to be considered incorrect. With all due respect, I strongly disagree. We must consider the other names to be incorrect since the name of letters in a language is a fundamental unifying element. However, I am completely in agreement with the Academy's suggested names:

- **b**, with its name **be** (pronounced like "bay" in English, without any need for any adjective afterwords)
- **v**, with its name **uve** (pronounced like "ooveigh" in English, without any need for any adjective afterwords)
- **w**, with the name **uve doble** (pronounced like "ooveigh dough-bleigh" in English)
- **y**, with the name **ye** (prunounced in English like "Yeigh")

To avoid confusion, I have decided not to include the unacceptable names that correspond with each letter. It is sufficient to say that the letter **b** has at least three unacceptable names, **v** has at least five, and that **w** has at least four. I really don't lose any sleep about the alternate name for the **y** in Castilian, just as I don't regarding the two different names that exist for the letter **z** in English. However, I do agree that the name proposed by the Academy is a good target.

I applaud the Taxis Libres company in Bogotá, Colombia, since in their automatic phone system, when they announce the license plate of the car that will pick up the client, they properly pronounce the letter **v** with the unified name **uve**. For some reason, I have heard some Colombians pronounce it as "uvé", emphasizing the last syllable, but that is not the unified pronunciation that the Academy and I am proposing. The unified name is **uve**, with emphasis on the second to last* syllable, and that's exactly how Taxis Libres' system says it.

*In Castilian, for the purposes of accentuation and stressed syllables, they are counted from the end of the word backwards, not from the beginning forward.

The Castilian alphabet as it is used in radio/TV advertising in the United States

It is unfortunate, but in many Castilian-language radio and TV spots in the United States, the announcers read the letters in acronyms in English. This is both damaging and insulting. That's why I insist to advertisers in the US: When the ad is in Castilian and includes acronyms, spell out the letters with their names in Castilian! Whether we work in journalism or in advertising, as professional communicators, we have the responsibility to present the best example to the public. (The only possible exception would be in an acted scene, where logically *Costumbrismo* is allowed... but never when "the firm" is speaking.)

26

THE VERB HAY: UNIQUE IN ITS CATEGORY

The conjugated verb *hay* (pronounced like the English word "eye", and meaning "There is" or "There are") is unique in its category, well almost. I say that because although it is evidently linked to the infinitive *haber* (to have, used in perfect tenses) in its formation and conjugation, according to the rules, *hay* should never, ever be pluralized. In the present indicative, it is *hay*, both in singular and plural and nobody misconjugates it:

- *Hay un libro.* (There is one book.)
- *Hay dos libros.* (There are two books.)

I don't know about many languages, but at least in Italian this is not the case, since it would be:

- *C'è un libro.*
- *Ci sono due libri.*

Something strange happened with the verb *hay*, not only because it doesn't vary between singular and plural in the present indicative, but also —by rule— it should never, ever be pluralized in the present subjunctive. For example:

- *Quiero que haya un milagro esta tarde.* (I want there to be a miracle this afternoon.)
- *Quiero que haya dos milagros esta tarde.* (I want there to be two miracles this afternoon.)

Or in the present indicative:

- *No hubo ninguna colombiana en la fiesta.* (There wasn't a single Colombian woman at the party.)
- *Hubo tres bellas colombianas en la fiesta.* (There were three beautiful Colombian women at the party.)

Nor in the imperfect indicative:

- *En la casa donde me crié había un árbol...* (In the house where I grew up there was a tree...)
- *En la casa donde me crié había tres árboles...* (In the house where I grew up there were three trees...)

... and so on in all tenses and modes. However, this rule tends to fight the nature of many native speakers to want to pluralize the verb *hay* in all tenses and verbs outside the present indicative. By nature, the speaker wants to say (and write):

- Quiero que hayan dos milagros esta tarde.
- Hubieron tres bellas colombianas en la fiesta.
- En la casa donde me crié habían tres árboles...

And then the overcorrection pops up: Somebody comes along and says: "You should never, ever say *hubieron*." But that is false. You may and must properly say *hubieron* not when it is the preterite of *hay*, but the preterite of *han*, to form the very seldom used preterite version of the past perfect, for example *hubieron visto*. I reiterate that it is extremely seldom used (*Habían visto* is much more frequent.) but it does exist and it's valid, and of course, *hubieron visto* is completely different from the subjunctive *hubieran visto*, which is frequently used.

27

JUGO OR ZUMO? PAPAS OR PATATAS?

In the Américas, Castilian speakers call **juice** *jugo*, and they generally call **potatoes** *papas*. In Spain, Castilian speakers generally call them *zumo* and *patatas* respectively. Just as Vicente Fox pointed out to us earlier in this book, there is large number of regional terms. This produces a challenge for writers and translators when our goal is to create a message that is intelligible for an international Castilian-speaking audience. As a writer and translator, this challenge has come up countless of times. Naturally, we use the most unified and widely understood terminology, so that the maximum number of consumers can be able to understand it in the maximum number of places. However, we have observed that the linguistic gap is greater between the Americas and Spain then between Castilian-language countries of the Americas. Here are just a few examples.

- *jugo* (Americas)/ *zumo* (Spain)

- *plomero* (Americas)/ *fontanero* (Spain) (**plumber** in both cases)

In my experience, these two examples are usually unintelligible in the opposite region.

The challenge is even greater when you have to make an audible presentation, as we cover in the next chapter.

28

THE NEED FOR BI-REGIONAL AUDIOBOOKS AND DUBBING

The bi-regionality of audiobooks and dubbing bring advantages to authors, narrators, and listeners.

Whether we like it or not, the majority of Castilian speakers in the Americas prefer to listen to audiobooks narrated by a narrator from the Americas and will not tolerate listening to one from Spain for several consecutive hours (although there are exceptions to that preference). Similarly, the majority of Spaniards won't tolerate listening to a narrator from the Americas for several consecutive hours (although again, there are exceptions to that preference). I know this after many conversations with many people from both regions. That's why I have come to the conclusion that in order to achieve good sales in each region, there must be two versions produced of each audiobook, one for each region. The same thing happens with dubbed movies and that's why they are often dubbed bi-regionally. The only positive difference in the case of audiobooks is that at least there is no segregation in the distribution. So when someone from the Americas prefers a narration made by a Spaniard, the option will be available. The reverse also occurs in Spain, since the purchase and download is available in both versions.

In the case of audiobooks, because of the fact that there must be a matching Kindle (digital text) book for each audiobook, it is necessary —for the first time— to have two versions of every Kindle book in order to have a pair the audiobook for the particular region. One of them is named in the format: **Title** (*versión para las Américas*) and that's how it appears in the Amazon, Audible and Apple Books stores. Later, the second version is labeled as **Title** (*versión para España*). Before the audiobook explosion and pairing, authors fought to write in a unified Castilian. However, given this new situation, now we must do the opposite in order to justify the existence of two different Kindle versions for each title. So far, I have already coordinated the production of several Kindle books prepared that way for authors/clients, and I've also coordinated their respective bi-regional audiobooks.

Speaking of exceptions to the rule, I do appreciate audiobooks that are narrated by both Spaniards and from narrators from the Americas. In fact, the Spanish Constitution is available as an audiobook narrated by my friend Victoria Mesas García, of the EscuchaLibros.com production company, from Spain. Of course, her recording includes the section of the Spanish Constitution that I quoted earlier in this book. It is available vía Audible.com and Apple Books. Also, Víctoria performed part of the opening from my online radio show, *CapicúaFM*. Another exception to this rule is when the actual author performs her/his own audiobook.

29
LATIN AMERICA, HISPANIC AMERICA, IBERO-AMERICA OR WHAT?

Although they often receive criticism, *América Latina*, **Latin America**, and *Latinoamérica* are popular names that are used to refer to regions where three Romance languages (or neo-Latin languages) are the majority. (Ahead I'll be defending one of them.)

First, many people who use the terms *América española*, *América hispana*, *Hispanoamérica*, and **Spanish América** define them as "a cultural region integrated by the American states where Spanish is spoken (sic)". Logically I reject these terms because —of course— there is no single Spanish language.

Second, **Iberoamerica** is a term made up of the words Iberia and America to designate a group of European and American territories where some Ibero Romance languages are spoken. Of all of these terms discussed so far in this chapter,

Iberoamérica is the most ambiguous one since there is debate as to whether to include or exclude the French language under the umbrella of Iberia.

Due to the controversy surrounding the terms *América Latina*, **Latin America**, and *Latinoamérica*, my personal rejection of *América española*, *América hispana*, *Hispanoamérica*, and **Spanish América** ... and the ambiguity of **Iberoamérica**, I prefer to adapt my personal use to the particular situation. I have found that most of the time, it's fine just to say **the Americas** since the context usually covers the rest. In those few cases when it is truly merited, I use *Castellanoamérica*, *castellanoamericana*, *castellanoamericano*, **Castilian America**, **Castilian America**, or **Castilian American**.

I fully recognize that **Latin America** (and *Latinoamérica* in Castilian) is the name of an important commercial region used by many international companies and really has no substitute. One example of that is my friend María Claudia Torres's official job title: Director of Demand Generation **Latin America** at NewTek. Another case is my friend Fernando Monetti, who is the Sales Director for **LatAm**. (**LatAm** is an acronym for **Latin America** which is often used in Castilian and English.) In these cases and many other similar ones, there is no other appropriate substitute. The reasons:

The second language in the US is indeed Castilian, but the United States is not part of Latin America. In fact, the United States is number 2 among all Castilian-speaking nations, thanks to our Castilian-speaking population. The number 1 Castilian-speaking country is México, the land of Vicente Fox.

30
THE PLURAL OF TÚ AND ITS RESPECTIVE BLACK HOLE

In standard Castilian, the second person singular is expressed in two different ways:

tú and *usted* (although the *usted* is conjugated as if it were the third person). In standard Castilian, *tú* (*tuteo*) is the informal pronoun (and treatment) that shows closeness and familiarity, while *usted* is more distant and is used in more formal situations where more respect is indicated. [There are some regions where these two treatments are occasionally reversed, in an ironic way. For example, I have met some people from Bogotá, Colombia that treat me as *tú*, while simultaneously treating their brothers or spouse as *usted*. These are exceptional uses that go beyond the scope of this chapter.] There are also regions in the Americas where *vos* is used as a singular second person treatment, which we will be covering ahead in this book.

The focus of this chapter is —as the title indicates—the plural of *tú* and its respective black hole in the Americas. In a completely illogical way, in the Americas, people tend to pluralize *tú* as *ustedes*. This practice unnecessarily inserts distance and lack of linguistic consistency when used with people that are normally treated individually as *tú*.

No. I am not going to propose the creation of a new pronoun. The pronoun already exists in Castilian, but it continues to be abandoned in the Americas. I am talking about the plural pronouns **vosotras** and **vosotros**. Even though these terms and conjugations are included in the curriculum in the Americas, its teaching has been extremely weak and haphazard. I affirm this because most of the Castilian speakers I've met from the Americas tend to use these pronouns when attempting to imitate Spaniards (quite poorly) —and to make things worse— they often use them when it is obvious that their real intention is to speak in singular, thus demonstrating their lack of familiarity about the true plural nature of these pronouns and respective conjugations. (Of course, I exclude from that observation my Castilian-speaking friends from the Americas that are language specialists, and they represent a small percentage of the public.)

Some Castilian speakers from the Americas have shown ill feelings about the **vosotras**/**vosotros** pronouns and treatment since they associate it with the Spanish conquest. I consider that association to be absurd. With that criteria, they should completely abandon the Castilian language. Evidently, those people have forgotten that the entire Castilian language that they use daily came from Spain, not just those two pronouns and their verb conjugations. They are cutting their nose to spite their face, since they are handicapping their primary communication tool —the Castilian language— for the sake of silly and illogical vengeance.

Others have inappropriately associated the **vosotras/vosotros** treatment with another era, like biblical language. That attitude without foundation in the current Global Village (thanks Marshall McLuhan). The **vosotras/vosotros** is not like the *thou* treatment in English, which has been abandoned worldwide except for marriage ceremonies and in the Bible. The **vosotras/vosotros** treatment is used daily by an estimate of 42.27 million Spaniards, according to the National Institute for Statistics (Spain) and the World Bank.

We are not talking about a regional preference for a particular word, as in Cuba where they like to call a license plate *chapa*, in Puerto Rico they prefer to call it *tablilla* (when the standard Castilian term is *placa*), and in the southernmost American countries they prefer to call an avocado *palta* instead of the more common *aguacate*. We are talking about a deficiency, a black hole, both a pair of pronouns and a verb conjugation that completes the *tú* format when dealing with more than one person. To pluralize *tú* as *ustedes* is illogical and unjustified, when the proper plural already exists. That's why I insist that institutes throughout the Americas take this treatment and conjugation more seriously, by including dialogs with exams that emphasize the differences between the singular and the plural. It is not necessary to imitate an Iberian accent to use this treatment and conjugation in the Americas. Only knowledge of the pronouns

vosotras/vosotros/vuestra/vuestro and **os**

are necessary, together with their conjugations in practical situations where the differences between plural and singular are obvious. Castilian speakers from the Americas have the right to have full access to the complete toolset their language offers, and should not be deprived.

31

ADVANTAGES OF TREATING PEOPLE AS TÚ

Whenever possible without being disrespectful, I like to use the *tú* form, and treat my readers and listeners in the singular, because of basic marketing term that states: Talk to one person.

Beyond that, there are other advantages to using the *tú* treatment in Castilian. Ahead you'll see an anecdote that has been well distributed via Internet, which clarifies another advantage. First you'll see the pure Castilian anecdote, followed by an adapted version in English with clarifications:

> El director general de un banco se preocupaba por un empleado que, después de un período de trabajar junto a él, sin parar nunca, ni para almorzar, empieza a ausentarse al mediodía. Entonces el director general del banco, preocupado que posiblemente el director esté robando al banco, llama a un detective privado y le dice:

- Siga a López una semana entera, no vaya a ser que ande en algo malo o sucio o que nos robe.

El detective cumple con el cometido, vuelve e informa:

- López sale normalmente al mediodía, toma su coche, va a su casa a almorzar, luego le hace el amor a su mujer, se fuma uno de sus excelentes habanos y vuelve a trabajar.

Responde el director:

-¡Ah, bueno! ¿Entonces no nos roba?

Entonces el detective pregunta:

-¿Puedo tutearlo, señor?

Sorprendido, el director responde:

-Sí, hombre, cómo no.

Y, entonces, el detective le dice:

- Te repito: López sale normalmente al mediodía, toma tu coche, va a tu casa a almorzar, luego le hace el amor a tu mujer, se fuma uno de tus excelentes habanos y vuelve a trabajar.

Here is the adaptation in English:

The general director of a bank is concerned because a relatively new employee, after a time of working there without stopping, not even for lunch, starts to go out of the bank at midday. Due to his concern that the guy might be embezzling, the director general of the bank hires a private detective and tells him:

- Follow López for a full week, and try to see if he does anything wrong or seems to be embezzling.

The detective fulfills the request and comes back to report:

- López typically leaves at midday; takes *su* car; goes to *su* house to eat lunch; later he makes passionate love to *su* wife; he smokes one of *sus* Havana cigars, and returns to work.

The director responds:

-Oh, good! He's not embezzling?

The detective asks:

-Sir, may I please treat you as *tú*?

Surprised, the director responds:

-Yes, no problem.

Then the detective tells him:

- I repeat: López typically leaves at midday; takes **your** car; goes to **your** house to eat lunch; later he makes passionate love to **your** wife; smokes one of **your** Havana cigars, and returns to work.

This was complex to adapt for English, but the issue is that the possessive adjective *su* can refer to anything from **her/his/its/yours**, while the possessive adjective *tu* (without any accent mark) can refer only to **yours**. So by treating him as *tú*, he was able to use the very specific *tu* possessive adjective, and the director finally understood.

(The story is anonymous.)

32

DOES IT BEHOOVE US TO TRANSLATE PROPER NAMES?

Some people insist that proper names should <u>never</u> be translated. However, many of those haven't noticed that the following have been translated for centuries (at least):

- Most European country names
- Most Bible characters
- Most Popes
- Many cartoons, children stores and their characters

Let's see some examples of each.

European countries

- Albania is called *Shqipëri* or *Shqipëria* in Albanian.
- Germany is called *Deutschland* in German and *Alemania* in Castilian.

- Finland is called *Suomi* in Finnish and in Swedish.
- Greece is called Ελλάς (Elláda) in Greek.
- England is called *Inglaterra* in Castilian.

Biblical characters

- Adam is called אָדָם in Hebrew, in Arabic, آدم and in Castilian, *Adán*.
- Moses is called מֹשֶׁה (Moshé) in Hebrew and in Castilian, *Moisés*.
- Jesus is called ישוע (Yeshua) in Hebrew and in Castilian *Jesús* (pronounced quite differently from English).

Popes

- Pope John Paul II (mentioned earlier in this book) is called *oannes Paulus II* in Latin, *Giovanni Paolo II* in Italian; *Jan Paweł II*; in Polish and in Castilian, *Papa Juan Pablo II*.
- Pope Francis is *Franciscus PP* in Latin and in Castilian, *Papa Francisco* (pronounced quite differently from English).

Cartoons, children stores and their characters

- The Flintstones in Castilian is called *Los Picapiedra*.
- The protagonist Fred Flintstone in Castilian is *Pedro Picapiedra*. (Although the last name is a translation, the first name is really a random choice.)
- His neighbor, Barney Rubble in Castilian is *Pablo Mármol*.

Stars' names from the entertainment field are not usually translated. Only if you were kidding would you translate Julio Iglesias's name as "July Churches". However, in all of the other cases shown above, they are generally translated. If you are among those who reject translating country names, I ask you: How many people will understand you if you ask: Do you speak *Suomi*? I remind you that *Suomi* is the English name of Finland and also the name of their language, Finnish, which in Castilian is called *finés*.

To the question which is the title of this chapter:

Does it behoove us to translate proper names?

My response is: Sometimes.

33
PROPER NAMES AND THEIR ALLOWABLE SPELLINGS

My colleague José Martínez de Sousa (whom I don't yet know personally yet) and I are both driven crazy when some individuals incorrectly declare that proper names are not subject to writing rules in Castilian. Actually, it gets more complex than that in Castilian, because of the terminology. What they say (unjustifiably) in Castilian is: "*Los nombres propios no tienen ortografía*" which essentially means that proper names are not subject to writing rules. Well they are and they aren't. Let's let José say it in his words, I'll adapt it, and then we'll continue.

...(Esto) no es exacto. Más acertado sería decir que cada apellido (o nombre) tiene su particular grafía, que en la mayor parte de los casos es semejante a la de los que tiene la misma formación, y en otros difiere: por ejemplo, una persona que se llame **Sánchez** se llama así y no Sanchez;

sin embargo, el apellido **Jiménez** adopta tres formas, por lo menos: **Jiménez, Giménez** o **Ximénez**. Aquí es obligatorio respetar la grafía peculiar de cada apellido; por ejemplo, si la persona lo escribe con G (**Giménez**), no debemos ponerle J (**Jiménez**), por más que también sea correcto. Resulta inadmisible que un señor que se llame **Martínez** dique que escribe sin acento en la **i**, entonces no sería palabra llana, sino aguda.

Adaptation/explanation:

...(This) is not exactly true. It would be more correct to say that every last name (or first name) has its own particular graphic rendering, which in the majority of cases is similar to other similar names, and in others is different: for example, a person named **Sánchez** is called as such and not Sanchez (without the accent mark, which would have the emphasis on the last syllable instead of the second to last); however, the last name **Jiménez** has at least three proper graphic renderings: **Jiménez, Giménez** or **Ximénez**. Here it is obligatory to respect the peculiar graphic rendering of each last name; for example, if the person writes it with a **G** (**Giménez**), we must not spell it with a **J** (**Jiménez**) even though it is correct for other people. It is inadmissible if a person named **Martínez** says that it is written without the accent mark. If he did, it would have the emphasis on the last syllable instead of the second to last.

Note: In Castilian, syllables are counted from the last syllable towards the front.

The other related detail —that José explains better than anyone— is the case of foreign names and their proper spelling in Castilian. Here is his original, followed by adaptation.

> ...los apellidos (y nombres) extranjeros deben escribirse con la misma grafía de su lengua de origen... Sin embargo, cuando se trata de apellidos procedentes de lenguas cuyos alfabetos son distintos del latino (cirílico, griego, chino, etcétera), deben transcribirse a nuestra fonética, pero directamente, no a través de idiomas intermedios...

Adaptation/explanation:

> ... Foreign names must be written with the same graphic rendering as they were written in the foreign language... However, when we deal with names that come from languages that use a non-Latin alphabet (like Cyrillic, Greek, Chinese, etc.), we must transliterate them according to the Castilian phonetic system, but directly, not by using any intermediate language's phonetic system...

Both quotes are from his book *dudas y errores de lenguaje* (the name is written with an initial lower case letter at José's insistence), fifth edition 1992 editorial Paraninfo, pages 97 to 98. I highly recommend it if you don't have it yet (and read and write Castilian).

34

UNITED STATES CITIES AND THEIR OFFICIAL SPELLINGS IN CASTILIAN

Several cities (and states) in the United States have their official spellings in Castilian, which I applaud. Here are some examples with their English name followed by their established Castilian spelling:

- Buffalo>*Búfalo*
- Philadelphia>*Filadelfia*
- Indianapolis>*Indianápolis*
- Minneapolis>*Mineápolis*
- Missouri>*Misuri*
- New York>*Nueva York*
- North Carolina>*Carolina del norte*
- Pennsylvania>*Pensilvania*
- South Carolina>*Carolina del sur*

Of the mentioned names, some are translations while others are Castilianizations, so both phenomena exist with geographical locations in the United States.

Why are two important South Florida cities missing from the list (where I have lived) like Coral Gables and Miami? For many years, whenever I write in Castilian, I write them as *Gabletes Coralinos* and *Mayami*. In the first case, it's a translation and in the second it's a restored Castilanization (I was not the Castilianizer in this case, just the restorer). Let's go case by case.

Gabletes Coralinos

Sadly, most people who live in the City of Coral Gables have no idea what the name means. When I first arrived there, I asked my friend Anthony Palomo and he explained it to me. Later I verified the word **gable** and *gablete* in their respective dictionaries and he was correct.

In English, a gable is triangular ornament placed between the edges of a sloping roof. According to the story, typical houses in Coral Gables had their gable made out of coral extracted from the sea.

Here is the definition of *gablete* at RAE.es

(Del fr. gablet).

1. m. Arq. Remate formado por dos líneas rectas y ápice agudo, que se ponía en los edificios de estilo ojival.

. . .

Mayami

The name of this city comes from an an indigenous name. If you'll recall your history, the first Europeans to arrive to these lands were Spaniards who spoke Castilian. Since the indigenous groups who lived here did not write with the Latin alphabet, the Spaniards who arrived here logically followed José Martínez de Sousa's rule to the letter (the one we covered in the previous chapter of this book) and wrote it the way it sounded, and encoded it using the Castilian códec. Initially, they wrote it a longer way (*Mayaimi*) and later they shortened it to *Mayami*. At first, even the anglos copied the Castilian spelling and before creating the current English spelling. But if we follow the logic of José Martínez de Sousa's rule, we must restore and maintain the original Castilian spelling (of course, simplified to *Mayami*) when writing it in Castilian.

Even though I have dared to translate *Gabletes Coralinos* and rescue the original *Mayami* spelling, that's not enough. The respective city halls should decree the official Castilian name, just as there are already official Castilian spellings for the other place we already discussed: *Búfalo*, *Filadelfia*, *Indianápolis*, *Misuri*, *Nueva York*, *Carolina del Norte*, Carolina del sur, and *Pensilvania*. The cities of Coral Gables and Miami deserve their official Castilian spellings just as much as the other places do.

If the mayors of these cities are wondering if there is any legal precedent for changing a city's name, the answer is affirmative: they should just look at the city of **Bogotá**, Colombia, where the government has changed it back and forth between **Santafé de Bogotá** or **Santa Fe de Bogotá** and simply Bogotá.

Correction of Coral Gables street names

In Coral Gables, many of the street names are in Castilian, but in many cases, unfortunately they are missing their accent mark or ñ/Ñ on the signs. City hall must correct the spelling of these names on their signs. Some of the ones that come to mind are **Castañeda** (which happens to be my friend Tanya's last name), **Ponce de León**, and **Santoña**. In the neighboring city of Miami Beach, they added the ñ on the street sign of **Española Way**, so what's preventing Coral Gables from doing the same? Writing the names haphazardly in Castilian is no good. It must be complete!

THE SINGULAR VOS

As an alternative to the *tú* which we covered previously in this book, many countries in the Americas use the singular *vos*. Some people incorrectly believe that the *vos* is used in few countries, when in reality, there are more Castilian American countries than those that don't. Countries that use it include:

- Argentina
- Bolivia
- Colombia (paisa and Cali areas)
- Costa Rica
- Ecuador
- El Salvador
- Honduras
- Guatemala
- Nicaragua
- Paraguay

- Uruguay
- Venezuela (Maracaibo, Zulia)

Vos is an informal second person singular pronoun, and is used as an alternative to the *tú* (or sometimes to show more closeness than the *tú*). Some people confuse the *vos* pronoun with the **vosotras/vosotros** pronouns that are frequently used in Spain (which we covered in detail earlier in this book). However, **vosotras/vosotros** are plural, not singular. So **vosotras/vosotros** are the plurals of *vos*, although ironically, there is no country where the combination **vos>vosotras** or **vos>vosotros** is popularly used. In Spain the singular of **vosotras/vosotros** is *tú*, while in the Americas, *ustedes* is illogically used as the plural of *tú* (as covered in detail earlier in this book).

Unfortunately, the *vos* pronoun and conjugation are not generally included in the curriculum, not even in countries that use it. (The Royal Academy does include conjugations for the singular *vos* in the indicative, but not in the subjunctive. However, in this book you'll get the full conjugation.)

This fact causes several negative repercussions:

1. Many people incorrectly believe that the *vos* pronoun and conjugation are not acceptable or proper. (They are both acceptable and proper, as long as the conjugation is correct.)
2. Many people are unfamiliar with the proper conjugation. For example, in Buenos Aires, they generally conjugate it correctly in the indicative, but

incorrectly in subjunctive (with the notable exception of verbs of the first conjugation, those that end with **ar**, where they sometimes conjugate them correctly, and sometimes not). In Maracaibo, Zulia, Venezuela, they unfortunately use the singular *vos* with the **vosotras/vosotros** (plural) conjugation, which causes much confusion.

Voseo puro:

	ACOSTARSE			MOLER			CONTRIBUIR	
Yo	me acuesto		Yo	muelo		Yo	contribuyo	
Tú Vos	te acuestas te acostás	Vosotras Vosotros	os acostáis	Tú Vos	mueles molés	Vosotras Vosotros	moléis	Tú Vos	contribuyes contribuís	Vosotras Vosotros	contribuís
Él Ella Usted	se acuesta	Ellos Ellas Ustedes	se acuestan	Él Ella Usted	muele	Ellos Ellas Ustedes	muelen	Él Ella Usted	contribuye	Ellos Ellas Ustedes	contribuyen
Presente del subjuntivo			**Presente del subjuntivo**			**Presente del subjuntivo**		
Yo	me acueste		Yo	muela		Yo	contribuya	
Tú Vos	te acuestes te acostés	Vosotras Vosotros	os acostéis	Tú Vos	muelas molás	Vosotras Vosotros	moláis	Tú Vos	contribuyas contribuyás	Vosotras Vosotros	contribuyáis
Él Ella Usted	se acueste	Ellos Ellas Ustedes	se acuesten	Él Ella Usted	muela	Ellos Ellas Ustedes	muelan	Él Ella Usted	contribuya	Ellos Ellas Ustedes	contribuyan
Imperativo:			**Imperativo**			**Imperativo**		
Tú Vos	acuéstate acostate	Vosotras Vosotros	acostaos	Tú Vos	muele molé	Vosotras Vosotros	moled	Tú Vos	contribuye contribuí	Vosotras Vosotros	contribuid
Usted	acuéstese	Ustedes	acuéstense	Usted	muela	Ustedes	muelan	Usted	contribuya	Ustedes	contribuyan
Imperativo negativo:			**Imperativo negativo:**			**Imperativo negativo:**		
Tú Vos	no te acuestes no te acostés	Vosotras Vosotros	no os acostéis	Tú Vos	no muelas no molás	Vosotras Vosotros	no moláis	Tú Vos	no contribuyas no contribuyás	Vosotras Vosotros	no contribuyáis
Usted	no se acueste	Ustedes	no se acuesten	Usted	no muela	Ustedes	no muelan	Usted	no contribuya	Ustedes	no contribuyan

Voseo maracucho:

	ACOSTARSE		
Yo	me acuesto	Nosotras/Nosotros	Nos acostamos
Tú / Vos	te acuestas / te acostáis	Vosotras/Vosotros	os acostáis
Él/Ella/Usted	se acuesta	Ellos/Ellas/Ustedes	se acuestan
Presente del subjuntivo			
Yo	me acueste	Nosotras/Nosotros	nos acostemos
Tú / Vos	te acuestes / te acostéis	Vosotras/Vosotros	os acostéis
Él/Ella/Usted	se acueste	Ellos/Ellas/Ustedes	se acuesten
Imperativo:			
Tú / Vos	acuéstate / acostate	Vosotras/Vosotros	acostaos
Usted	acuéstese	Ustedes	acuéstense
Imperativo negativo:			
Tú / Vos	no te acuestes / no te acostéis	Vosotras/Vosotros	no os acostéis
Usted	no se acueste	Ustedes	no se acuesten

	MOLER		
Yo	muelo	Nosotras/Nosotros	molemos
Tú / Vos	mueles / moléis	Vosotras/Vosotros	moléis
Él/Ella/Usted	muele	Ellos/Ellas/Ustedes	muelen
Presente del subjuntivo			
Yo	muela	Nosotras/Nosotros	molamos
Tú / Vos	muelas / moláis	Vosotras/Vosotros	moláis
Él/Ella/Usted	muela	Ellos/Ellas/Ustedes	muelan
Imperativo			
Tú / Vos	muele / molé	Vosotras/Vosotros	moled
Usted	muela	Ustedes	muelan
Imperativo negativo:			
Tú / Vos	no muelas / no moláis	Vosotras/Vosotros	no moláis
Usted	no muela	Ustedes	no muelan

	CONTRIBUIR		
Yo	contribuyo	Nosotras/Nosotros	contribuimos
Tú / Vos	contribuyes / contribuís	Vosotras/Vosotros	contribuís
Él/Ella/Usted	contribuye	Ellos/Ellas/Ustedes	contribuyen
Presente del subjuntivo			
Yo	contribuya	Nosotras/Nosotros	contribuyamos
Tú / Vos	contribuyas / contribuyáis	Vosotras/Vosotros	contribuyáis
Él/Ella/Usted	contribuya	Ellos/Ellas/Ustedes	contribuyan
Imperativo			
Tú / Vos	contribuye / contribuí	Vosotras/Vosotros	contribuid
Usted	contribuya	Ustedes	contribuyan
Imperativo negativo:			
Tú / Vos	no contribuyas / no contribuyáis	Vosotras/Vosotros	no contribuyáis
Usted	no contribuya	Ustedes	no contribuyan

For example, if someone from Maracaibo attempts to invite a single person in a group by saying: "*¿Queréis ir al cine?*" it is very likely that everyone present will think they were included in the invitation.

Voseo porteño:

	ACOSTARSE		MOLER		CONTRIBUIR	
Yo	me acuesto	Yo	muelo	Yo	contribuyo	Nosotras Nosotros
Tú Vos	te acuestas te acostás	Tú Vos	mueles molés	Tú Vos	contribuyes contribuís	Vosotras Vosotros
Él Ella Usted	se acuesta	Él Ella Usted	muele	Él Ella Usted	contribuye	Ellos Ellas Ustedes
Presente del subjuntivo:		**Presente del subjuntivo::**		**Presente del subjuntivo:**		
Yo	me acueste	Yo	muela	Yo	contribuya	Nosotras Nosotros
Tú Vos	te acuestes (ver comentario)	Tú Vos	muelas muelas	Tú Vos	contribuyas contribuyás	Vosotras Vosotros
Él Ella Usted	se acueste	Él Ella Usted	muela	Él Ella Usted	contribuya	Ellos Ellas Ustedes
Imperativo:		**Imperativo:**		**Imperativo:**		
Tú Vos	acuéstate acostate	Tú Vos	muele molé	Tú Vos	contribuye contribuí	Vosotras Vosotros
Usted	acuéstese	Usted	muela	Usted	contribuya	Ustedes
Imperativo negativo:		**Imperativo negativo:**		**Imperativo negativo:**		
Tú Vos	no te acuestes (ver comentario)	Tú Vos	no muelas no muelas	Tú Vos	no contribuyas no contribuyás	Vosotras Vosotros
Usted	no se acueste	Usted	no muela	Usted	no contribuya	Ustedes

Additional forms (Nosotras/Nosotros, Vosotras/Vosotros, Ellos/Ellas/Ustedes rows):

Pronouns	ACOSTARSE	MOLER	CONTRIBUIR
Nosotras/Nosotros	Nos acostamos	molemos	contribuimos
Vosotras/Vosotros	os acostáis	moléis	contribuís
Ellos/Ellas/Ustedes	se acuestan	muelen	contribuyen
Nosotras/Nosotros (subj.)	nos acostemos	molamos	contribuyamos
Vosotras/Vosotros (subj.)	os acostéis	moláis	contribuyáis
Ellos/Ellas/Ustedes (subj.)	se acuesten	muelan	contribuyan
Vosotras/Vosotros (imp.)	acostaos	moled	contribuid
Ustedes (imp.)	acuéstense	muelan	contribuyan
Vosotras/Vosotros (imp. neg.)	no os acostéis	no moláis	no contribuyáis
Ustedes (imp. neg.)	no se acuesten	no muelan	no contribuyan

Although the residents of Buenos Aires (known as *porteños*), Argentina, use the *vos* conjugations correctly when speaking in indicative mode, that's not the case in the present subjunctive or with the negative imperative. In those cases, they usually conjugate the *vos* with the *tú* conjugation. They even use the verb *tutear* when they really mean *vosear* (which has nothing to do with the verb *boxear* from boxing, the combat sport). But we love them anyway!

Using the *vos* is not an "accent" or tonality: It is a treatment that can be used with the "accent" of any particular region. I once asked a good Colombian friend why she didn't use the *vos*, even though she grew up in a city known for its use (Cali). She responded saying that she didn't like the "accent" of that city. Later I clarified that if she wants, she can use the *vos* and its conjugations together with her preferred accent.

36

WHY DO I ACCENT MY LAST NAME?

I accent my last name (Tépper) because before I did it, I had difficulties when many Castilian speakers mispronounced it. They used to pronounce it as if it were a verb, with emphasis on the final syllable. Ever since I added the accent mark, the problem disappeared. To my knowledge, I am the first Tépper to use the accent mark so far.

37

HAPPY BIRTHDAY IS NOT THE SAME AS FELIZ CUMPLEAÑOS

They lied to us when they told us that *¡Feliz cumpleaños!* is the exact translation of **Happy Birthday**, or vice versa. In reality, **Happy Birthday** would literally translate as *¡Feliz natalicio!*

In English, the linguistic focus is on the celebration of the anniversary of the birth, not the act of turning another year. In Castilian, the focus is on turning another year.

So what would be the proper translation of *¡Feliz cumpleaños!* in English? Of course, it would be **Happy Turnday!**

Why does this matter so much?

In Castilian, dead people (like historical figures) cannot have a *cumpleaños*, since they no longer *turn* another year. Instead they have their *natalicio* (anniversary of their birth date). In English, both living beings and dead people have their birthday (birth day).

38

SOME DREAMS COME TRUE...

Both in English and in Castilian, the word **dreams** (or *sueños*) refers both to wishes or goals, and to successions of images, ideas, emotions, and sensations that occur involuntarily in the mind during certain stages of sleep. In this chapter, I'm going to give you one of one type, and several of the other.

The dream I had when I was sleeping

At the beginning of this dream, I was walking on a sidewalk, very close the the building where my friend Carlos Matamoros had his office. As I walked, I saw a cat which was limping as it tried to continue to go forward. I got close, and saw that it was injured. I felt very sympathetic to the cat and picked it up in my hands to see if I could help it. (Remember, this was a dream.) When I picked it up and turned it around, I saw that its abdomen was cut, but instead of seeing guts and blood, I saw electronic components: transistors, potentiometers, chips, and blinking LEDs. It wasn't a toy, but a bionic cat!

For a long time, I asked myself what the dream might mean, without reaching any conclusion. I mentioned it to several friends, and finally Anthony Palomo made an excellent analysis and interpretation. Why did I feel so moved to help a poor cat? Why an injured cat, and why bionic? According to Anthony, the cat for me represents the Castilian language. It is logical, after the great cat incident that changed my life at eight years old and catapulted me to learn the language. (That was covered in the Introduction of this book, in case you missed it.) Anthony continued explaining that the cat was injured because for decades I have observed myths, conspiracies and misspellings related to the Castilian language and that's why the cat was vulnerable. He said that I bent down to help the cat for the same reason that I fight to protect the Castilian language from all of its attacks. Finally, Anthony clarified that the cat was bionic because I work with technology and because many of my Castilianizations have been techy. Thank you Anthony!

Some dreams (goals) I see for Castilian

- All colleges, institutes, schools, and universities worldwide must correct their nomenclature for the Castilian language.
- The Royal Academy (Real Academia Española) must

restore the appropriate, proper, and dignified name of its Dictionary: *Diccionario castellano de la Real Academia Española.*
- The few governments which got it wrong —Cuba, Guatemala, and Panamá— must correct their respective Constitutions so they indicate Castilian (*castellano*) as the official language.
- The respective city halls from Coral Gables and Miami must decree their official names in Castilian (*Gabletes Coralinos* and *Mayami*)... and in Coral Gables, they must fix the street names to include the missing accent marks and ñ/Ñs.
- The US government must activate the accent marks and ñ/Ñ in the permissible names in US passports. It is ironic to observe that while currently, ñ/Ñ and accent marks are rejected on passport names, the actual passport includes accent marks elsewhere, and at least postage stamp in the US includes an accent mark.
- Apple, Google, Microsoft and other software manufacturers must properly classify Castilian in all language lists.
- All colleges, institutes, schools, and universities worldwide that teach Castilian must make a serious effort when covering the singular *vos* and the plural *vosotras/vosotros*, including all of their respective conjugations, so that the students will be completely conscious of the versatility of the language that they speak (or are learning to speak).

¡Viva el castellano! Long Live Castilian!

Long Live the other Spanish languages too!

ABOUT THE AUTHOR

Born in Connecticut, United States, Allan Tépper is an award-winning broadcaster & podcaster, bilingual consultant, multi-title author, tech journalist, certified translator, and language activist who has been working with professional audio/video since the eighties. Since 1994, Tépper has been consulting both end-users and manufacturers through his Florida company. Via TecnoTur, Tépper has been giving video tech seminars in several South Florida's universities and training centers, and in a half dozen Latin American countries, in their native language. Tépper has been a frequent radio/TV guest on several radio and TV stations in Guatemala, Spain, US and Venezuela. As a certified ATA (American Translators Association) translator, Tépper has translated and localized dozens of advertisements, catalogs, software, and technical manuals for the Spanish and Latin American markets. He has also written many contracted white papers for tech manufacturers. Over the past 18 years, Tépper's articles have been published or quoted in more than a dozen magazines, newspapers, and electronic media. Since 2008, Allan Tépper's articles have been published frequently –in English– in *ProVideo Coalition* magazine.

Subscribe to free news at bulletins.AllanTepper.com or visit, AllanTepper.com, BeyondPodcasting.com or radio.AllanTepper.com to find out about his radio shows.

SOME OTHER BOOKS BY ALLAN TÉPPER

Some books in Castilian (the most widely used of all Spanish languages, worldwide):

- *Chromebooks para escritores bilingües*
- *El encubrimiento de la Real Academia*
- *La conspiración del castellano*

Some books In English:

- *Chromebooks for bilingual writers*
- *The Royal Spanish Coverup*
- *WordPress security + multi-backups*

Book in French:

- *Chromebooks pour écrivains bilingues* (translated by Séverine Torralba of SeveralTranslations.com)

This list is very incomplete. To see a more complete list, visit books.AllanTepper.com or libros.AllanTepper.com.

CREDITS, BRANDS, AND DISCLOSURES

FTC disclosure

Allan Tépper is the director of TecnoTur LLC. None of the companies listed in this book have paid Allan Tépper to appear in this book, although some of them have contracted Allan Tépper or TecnoTur LLC for professional services, or vice versa. Some affiliate links within this book may benefit Allan Tépper or TecnoTur LLC.

Photographs and portraits

- The portrait of Andrés Bello is public domain, author unknown.
- The photos of the author (Allan Tépper) are by Ángela Toro Tamayo and Konstanze Pelargus.
- The photo of Ilan Chester is courtesy of himself.

- The portrait of Antonio de Nebrija is public domain, courtesy of his children.
- The photo of Pope John Paul II is public domain, courtesy of Rob Croes (ANEFO) - This file has been extracted from another file: JohannesPaulusSimonis1985.jpg, Creative Commons 4.0.
- The photo of Vicente Fox Quesada is in public domain, courtesy of the Mexican government's *Noticias e Información de la Presidencia*.
- The photo of the *Diccionario de la lengua Castellana compuesto por la Real Academia Española* is used under the free GNU license. Thanks to Rhurtadon for that photo.
- The photos of the other dictionaries were taken by Allan Tépper.

Brands

All brands mentioned in this book belong to their respective owners.

Graphic consulting

Andreína Ascanio Toro

Revisions

Mónica Melamid

Aldo Zypce

www.ingramcontent.com/pod-product-compliance
Lightning Source LLC
Chambersburg PA
CBHW071350080526
44587CB00017B/3039